The Chero...

of the

Smoky Mountains

A Little Band that has stood against the White Tide for Three Hundred Years

Rewritten from the Papers of Horace Kephart author of

Our Southern Highlanders
&
Camping and Woodcraft

with an introduction by
Dr. John Finger

Printed in Canada

Three oddly related elements have combined to produce this little book: a largely forgotten remnant of a once great Indian tribe; a troubled man who found a new life in the Great Smoky Mountains; and a widow, living on the edge of poverty, who hoped to earn a few dollars and honor her deceased husband.

The Indians are the Cherokees of the Smokies, past and present. At the time of their first contact with whites, the Cherokees were among the most numerous peoples in the Southeast, with perhaps 20,000-25,000 members in many villages scattered along the valleys of the southern Appalachians. During the colonial era they forged a mutually profitable alliance with English traders, especially those from South Carolina. The whites brought packtrains of goods from Tidewater and exchanged them for deerskins and Indian slaves captured by the Cherokees from their traditional enemies. Gradually the Cherokees and other tribes became more dependent on European goods, a fact the English and French were quick to exploit.

The Cherokees usually supported Britain in her colonial wars with France, but occasionally, because of mutual aggravations, they exploded in violence against their trading partners. If they had analyzed the situation with the advantage of our hindsight, they would have perceived that Britain posed a greater threat, for her colonies required more and more land for their burgeoning populations. Always it was the land that drew the frontiersmen onward, in open defiance both of British regulations and Indian occupancy. Invoking the Biblical injunction to be fruitful, multiply, and subdue the earth, they insisted that no heathen Indians should be allowed to defy God's will.

When the American Revolution began, the Cherokees were quick to support the British as the only bulwark against the frontiersmen's encroachment. In retaliation, colonial militia units destroyed a number of Indian villages, but for more than a decade after the Revolution there were intermittent raids against the settlers. Not until the

1790s were the Cherokees completely pacified. By then the United States government was embarking upon a new program of "civilizing" the Indian by encouraging—and forcing—him to live more like whites. This included instruction in white agricultural techniques, conversion to Christianity, learning to read and write, and forsaking tribal landholding patterns. Such changes would have obvious advantages, for the more "settled" the Indians became the more land would be available for white expansion. This dual objective became the dominant theme of American Indian policy.

Of all the tribes that adapted to white ways, the Cherokees have long been viewed as the most successful. During the early nineteenth century Protestant missionaries established schools among them and converted many to Christianity. Many abandoned their towns and settled in log cabins on small farms, practicing a subsistence agriculture and appearing to live much like their white counterparts. Some of the more acculturated mixed-bloods occupied lovely homes, owned slaves, farmed hundreds of acres for a market economy, and invested in stores, mills, tanneries, and ferries. Sequoyah, a Cherokee genius, devised a unique syllabary so that his people could learn to read and write in their own language. Many did so. The tribe even had its own newspaper, the *Cherokee Phoenix*. A small number of influential individuals established a political system modeled on that of the United States, and by 1827 the Cherokee Nation could boast of a constitution and legislative, executive, and judicial bodies. These outward changes were impressive, but scholars have recently questioned just how far they extended beyond the politically and economically dominant mixed-bloods.

Regardless of whether the Cherokees were becoming more "civilized," white southerners were increasingly vociferous in demanding their removal to the West. The state of Georgia was especially insistent on this matter and eventually defied existing federal treaties by extending state laws over the Cherokees, incorporating their lands within newly organized counties, and generally making life difficult for them. President Andrew Jackson had the same objectives as Georgia's political leaders and, through persuasion, coercion, and chicanery, was able to remove most of the eastern tribes. The fate of the Cherokee Nation was sealed by a fraudulent treaty negotiated with a tiny tribal minority at New Echota, Georgia in December 1835. After it was ratified in May 1836, the Cherokee Nation had two years to move to a new homeland in present-day Oklahoma. When the vast majority of Cherokees had refused to budge by the spring of 1838, the United States Army enforced their removal westward over the Trail of Tears. About 16,000 left, never to return; perhaps 4,000 of them died on the trail.

Not surprisingly, many scholars and popular writers have depicted the events leading up to removal and the agony that accompanied the trek westward. As far as most people are concerned, the Cherokees' history in the Southeast ended with the removal of 1838. Nevertheless,

about fourteen hundred Cherokees managed to remain in remote corners of Georgia, North Carolina, Tennessee, and Alabama. Some were eventually absorbed into the dominant white population, but those in the mountains of western North Carolina had always been among the most traditional of their tribe and stubbornly retained their Indian identity. Eventually, after the Civil War, they coalesced into the Eastern Band of Cherokees, a corporate body recognized by both the federal and state governments. Through luck, perseverance, influential friends, and the fact that their mountain fastness offered few attractions to white farmers, these Indians were able to acquire and retain a large block of land known as the Qualla Boundary Reservation. Smaller units of the tribal domain are scattered through other parts of western North Carolina. Today there are more than 5,000 members of the Band residing on these lands. The center of tribal life is the town of Cherokee, situated along the Oconaluftee River and locked in a symbiotic embrace with the nearby Great Smoky Mountains National Park. Together they help sustain a tourist industry that has become the economic mainstay of the Indians and many neighboring whites.

Until the park was officially created in 1934, relatively few outsiders had broached the Cherokees' isolation and fewer yet had written anything about them. The most noteworthy exception was James Mooney, a young ethnologist who visited the eastern Cherokees in the 1880s and 1890s. His account of their history, life, and beliefs appeared in "Myths of the Cherokee", published in 1900 as part of the *Nineteenth Annual Report* of the Bureau of American Ethnology. Because of its ethnographic detail and historical data, "Myths of the Cherokee" quickly became a classic. Virtually every twentieth-century account of the Cherokees owes a large debt to it. Among those who liberally borrowed from Mooney was Horace Sowers Kephart, the author of the present booklet. Kephart was an individual of wide-ranging intellect who in his early

years betrayed no sign of the inner malaise that was to reshape his life. Born in Pennsylvania in September 1862, he spent his youth on the Iowa frontier, was educated at several colleges and universities, and embarked upon a promising career as a librarian-scholar.

During 1885-86 he lived in Florence, Italy, cataloging a collection of fourteenth-century Italian literature; his occasional walking trips in the Alps and Apennines imbued him with a love of mountains that was to become manifest in his later years. After returning to America, he translated some of Dante's work into English and taught himself enough Finnish to read the Finnish national epic in that language. More than a mere pedant, he humanized his studies by associating with immigrant enclaves of Italians and Finns, a direct approach to scholarly investigation that was to characterize his later work in Appalachia. In the meantime he was gaining professional respect as a librarian at Yale University. In April 1887 he married Laura Mack of Ithaca, New York, and seemed destined for a conventional academic and family life.

Dissatisfied with his chances for advancement at Yale, Kephart in 1890 accepted a position as director of the St. Louis Mercantile Library, where he helped compile one of the best collections on American frontier history. And there, amid the musty journals of long-dead mountain men and frontiersmen, he sniffed the air of adventure for the first time since his boyhood days in Iowa. In those pages he sensed exhilarating freedom—freedom from the pressures of civilization, time schedules, and family. He was also captivated by the romance and drama in Francis Parkman's sweeping account of wilderness warfare in the eighteenth century; he became familiar with Teddy Roosevelt's epic, *The Winning of the West*; with the writings of John Muir and other apostles of wilderness; familiar, too, with Frederick Jackson Turner's hypothesis that America owed its distinctiveness to the frontier. In the inner recesses of the Mercantile Library, Horace Kephart the adventurer and outdoorsman was born.

The catalyst for such a radical change was a deepening melancholy rooted in the emotional and economic demands of his growing family. Between 1888 and 1897, Laura bore him four daughters and two sons. Before long the middle-aged librarian was confronting what our own generation calls an "identity crisis." He became more withdrawn, less attentive to family, more susceptible to drink. His professional work deteriorated as he spent more and more time on solitary camping trips to the Ozark mountains and forests. His employers and family were distressed, and late in 1903, citing "ill health," he left his job and family. He would never return to either. Laura Kephart moved back to New York and raised the children herself, while her forty-one year old husband sought other directions.

Almost instinctively, Kephart perceived that his physical and psychic rejuvenation lay in a return to nature, to a simpler life located, as he put it, in a "Back of Beyond." His expert sleuthing in libraries convinced him that the least known, least written about areas in the eastern United States was the southern Appalachians. Traveling to western North Carolina, he resided for a few years in a cabin along a fork of Hazel Creek, on the rugged southern flank of the Smokies. It was about as far removed from twentieth-century civilization as one could be in the United States. Though he was hardly a recluse and periodically traveled, Kephart adopted the mountains as home and eventually settled in the little town of Bryson City, North Carolina. From 1904 until his death in 1931, the Appalachians offered the perfect environment for blending his inherent curiosity and scholarship with the maximum personal freedom. They became a part of him.

Kephart compiled twenty-seven volumes of systematically organized information on the flora, fauna, and people of the mountains (as well as miscellaneous other topics). In these, he would often make historical analogies and allude to obscure or ancient sources familiar only to scholars. Yet when he wrote for publication, he eschewed academic conventions and adopted a crisp, breezy, and humorous style that was utterly devoid of pretense. The melancholia that had afflicted him dissipated. As a self-taught expert in outdoor living, he earned enough money to meet his needs by writing scores of articles on such topics as hunting, fishing, rifles, ballistics, tenting, mountain lore, map-reading, and moonshining. Among the many magazines carrying his articles were *Sports Afield, Outing Magazine, Field and Stream, Boy's Life,* and even the *Ladies Home Journal.* His book *Camping and Woodcraft,* published in 1906, explained in concise terms the mysteries of outdoor America and how to cope with them in comfort. It became a bible for outdoorsmen and went through numerous revisions and reprintings. By the early 1920s Kephart the librarian had metamorphosed into one of the deans of outdoor writers and was dispensing genial advice as an editor of *Outing Magazine.*

But the work that made Kephart

known beyond a relatively few sportsmen was *Our Southern Highlanders*, published in 1913 by the Outing Publishing Company. With revisions, it has been republished several times by the MacMillan Company and, most recently, the University of Tennessee Press. Many still consider it the classic account of the southern mountains and their people. Kephart always took great satisfaction from the fact that mountaineers praised the book for its expert telling of their lives and folkways, right down to their dialects. After its publication, any outsider seeking to learn more about southern mountaineers would inevitably visit Horace Kephart at the Cooper boarding house in Bryson City. But despite its acclaim, the book was hardly a bestseller and brought its author only modest royalties.

In his later years Kephart became something of a patriarch of the southern Appalachians, enjoying a stature that led the United States Geographic Board to name a prominent peak of the Smokies after him. This and a small stream that originates on its slopes still bear his name. By the mid-1920s Kephart had reduced his commercial writing and was vigorously supporting creation of a national park in his beloved mountains. At the time of his death in an auto accident in April 1931 (returning from a mountain bootlegger), such a park seemed assured. When it became reality three years later, some North Carolinians viewed Kephart as its father.

Kephart's death at age sixty-eight was duly noted by newspapers throughout the nation. For his cronies, however, his passing meant something more than an obituary; it marked the loss of a powerful personality who had captured in print the heart and soul of Appalachia. Hundreds of people attended his funeral in Bryson City, but his friends viewed this interment as only temporary. What could be more fitting, they asked, than to bury "Kep" in the national park he had helped create? Despite their efforts during the next decade, the National Park Service, fearing a precedent, ultimately turned them down.

Nor were park authorities able to provide an appropriate museum for Kephart's papers and memorabilia. Today most of these are located at Western Carolina University and the Pack Memorial Library in Asheville. Anyone interested in published accounts of Kephart's life should consult Michael Frome's *Strangers in High Places: The Story of the Great Smoky Mountains*, and George Ellison's introduction to the 1976 edition of *Our Southern Highlanders* (University of Tennessee Press).

Among those attending Kephart's funeral were his long-estranged wife, two sons, and a grandson. For all the hurt she had suffered, Laura Kephart evinced no bitterness toward her less-than-dutiful husband. She had clearly liked the man, warts and all, and viewed his shortcomings as a consequence of his earlier illness rather than as a moral lapse or intentional wrong. She was proud of his popularity as a writer and seemed almost to use his prominence as justification for his having left her. She could believe that her sacrifices had served some larger purpose.

Kephart's children, in contrast, had almost nothing by which to judge the man. In the long years since he had left them, he had made little effort to maintain ties. As Laura later noted, the younger children could only vaguely recall their father, and the memories of the older ones were "not pleasant."

Some idea of the emotional distance separating Kephart and his children is revealed in a letter to him in 1921 from his son, Leonard. It is apparent that the two had only recently begun to correspond, and in response to his father's inquiry Leonard reported on his siblings, noting the years in which they had married and whether they had any children. During the last decade of his life, Kephart occasionally met or corresponded with his sons, but this was hardly a substitute for the missing years of paternal love and guidance.

Horace Kephart's death brings us to the posthumous publication of this booklet. Though he had been well aware of the Cherokees residing in the southern mountains (he passed through Qualla Boundary often),

Kephart alluded to them only briefly in *Our Southern Highlanders*. This was probably because he was preoccupied with establishing that the white highlanders were a homogenous people, lineal descendants of eighteenth-century Scots-Irish who, isolated from the currents of changing America, remained much as they had been in the colonial era; in certain respects, he believed, they had even regressed. The Cherokees, the original southern mountaineers, obviously did not fit into such a scheme. And so he wrote only a few articles on them, including one on their use of the blowgun and a series on "The Strange Story of the Eastern Cherokees" that appeared in the March, April, and May 1919 issues of *Outing Magazine*. In other works,he sometimes related anecdotes about Cherokees that today might be considered mildly racist but which in the Progressive Era seemed merely humorous. However, he paid more appropriate respect to them in "Smoky Mountain Magic," an unpublished novel which was still being revised at the time of his death [published in 2009 by Great Smoky Mountains Association]. In it he recognized their ancient residency in the Smokies, the tenacity of certain cultural traits, and the many injustices they had suffered. The present booklet, however, is Kephart's most accessible and complete account of the Cherokees, and it appeared only because of the combined efforts of his widow and Irving K. Stearns, the administrator of his estate.

Kephart's estate consisted mainly of letters, books, journals, clippings, and various camping paraphernalia. It was encumbered by a sizable debt, and about the only items of real or potential value were the manuscript of "Smoky Mountain Magic" and the royalties from *Our Southern Highlanders*. These assets eventually passed to Laura Kephart, who, like many Americans, was financially distressed during those dark days of the Depression. Stearns felt a commendable concern for her and suggested they try to find a publisher for "Smoky Mountain Magic." Because of the growing number of tourists visiting the Smokies, he thought there might also be a market for a brief treatise on the Cherokees. This could be prepared by combining Kephart's three articles on "The Strange Story of the Eastern Cherokees."

When Mrs. Kephart admitted her lack of business expertise, Stearns took time from his own company in Bryson City to seek out possible publishers. In a letter to the MacMillan Company, he briefly discussed the novel. Then, turning to the other project, he noted that Kephart had published the three-part series on the Cherokees and that Mrs. Kephart and he wanted

...to republish this in the form of a small book which will sell for 35¢ to 50¢ each in order to raise funds for the estate indebtedness. If you have any suggestions along this line or would care to go into the matter please let me know. For your information, quite a lot of the data was taken from the original Mooney ethnological report, with which you are no doubt familiar, and the illustrations are also from this work.

The MacMillan Company was interested in both projects but quickly decided against publishing "Smoky Mountain Magic." It appears that the publisher also rejected the Cherokee booklet, for in 1935 both Stearns and Laura Kephart were asking printers for estimates on the project. An Asheville firm offered to print 1,000 copies for $200, but the Atkinson Press of Ithaca, New York, won the contract by agreeing to print 2,000 copies for about $150. Mr. Atkinson was an "old neighbor" of Laura's and had watched her children grow up. She told Stearns that the extra 1,000 copies "can be used for kindling, if necessary," and that the savings in cost could pay for advertising. But publishing it would require all her limited resources, and she hoped the next royalty check from MacMillan for *Our Southern Highlanders* would help cover the costs.

In the fall of 1936 *The Cherokees of the Smoky Mountains* appeared as a thirty-six page, illustrated booklet under Laura Mack Kephart's copyright. According to the title page, the text was "Rewritten from the Papers of Horace Kephart." In truth, it was almost identical to the text of his three magazine articles of 1919. Mrs. Kephart had wanted to print it "just as Horace wrote it," but because she felt "a bit shaky about the legality" of reproducing the articles, she made "just enough change to protect a new copyright." Despite her lack of editorial experience, her changes generally improved the text.

Although the work was indisputably Horace Kephart's, it should be remembered that he had relied extensively on the works of James Mooney, Charles Royce, and other writers of the late nineteenth century. Kephart's history, then, reflects sources of almost one hundred years ago, and errors are to be expected. His story of the supposed martyrdom of Tsali, for example, comes directly from Mooney and requires substantial revision in light of evidence now available. His discussion of the Cherokees during the colonial period also contains errors. And historians of today are not as convinced as Kephart that Andrew Jackson was an "out-and-out Indian hater." But this is quibbling. Despite Kephart's occasional errors of fact and interpretation, scholars of today find his narration, emphases, and conclusions generally sound. It is perhaps enough for the general reader that Kephart tells the tale of the Eastern Cherokees boldly, clearly, and well.

An Asheville newspaper, in reporting the booklet's publication, said that visitors to the Cherokee reservation could now enjoy the only "readily available" account of early Cherokee history. Stearns served as Mrs. Kephart's loyal North Carolina agent, dutifully peddling copies to tourists and anyone else with an interest in Indians. She quickly recovered the printing costs but never earned more than a few extra dollars, partly because Stearns could not devote much time to the matter. In 1939 he said he was "hoping this will be a good tourist year, and if so, believe we will be able to dispose of some more booklets. I'll do my best but can't promise to spend a great deal of time." Later that year he admitted that he had sold only two or three copies. So it went during the next several years—only an occasional copy sold because, Stearns said, they needed "some promotional work by someone who has the time." After World War II most of the sales came through regional souvenir shops, museums, and historical associations. By the late 1970s *The Cherokees of the Smoky Mountains* had gone through a number of reprintings but without bringing much profit to the Kephart heirs.

Among the regional organizations that have sold the booklet are the Great Smoky Mountains Association, of Gatlinburg, Tennessee, a private organization which returns all profits to the Great Smoky Mountains National Park. Early in 1983 the association arranged with George S. Kephart (Horace's son) to reissue the booklet under its own imprimatur with this introduction and a new cover illustration. It is a repayment of sorts to Horace Kephart. Years ago the national park he had helped create had denied him burial within its boundaries and had been unable to create a museum for his papers and artifacts. Now, as the fiftieth birthday of that park approaches, it is appropriate to honor the man by republishing *The Cherokees of the Smoky Mountains*. Kephart would have appreciated both the recognition and the fact that, through this booklet, he continues to support the National Park.

John R. Finger

The University of Tennessee, Knoxville

John R. Finger is an Associate Professor of History at the University of Tennessee, Knoxville. A native Mid-westerner, he earned his degrees at the universities of Kansas and Washington. He has published a number of articles on the American westward movement and Indian-white relations. He is the author of The Eastern Band of Cherokees, 1819-1900, published by the University of Tennessee Press. An avid outdoorsman, he has spent much time in the Great Smoky Mountains and hiked many of the same trails as Horace Kephart.

The Cherokees
of the Smoky Mountains

In the southwestern corner of North Carolina is a band of Cherokee Indians. By a strange streak of fate, they alone, of a once powerful tribe, have been left in possession of a fragment of their ancient realm. They hold what is known as the Qualla boundary, about ninety square miles of rough country on the southerly slope of the Great Smoky Mountains. From time immemorial this natural fastness has been a refuge of their people in case of disaster.

The Cherokees are of Iroquoian stock or affinity, and apparently of northern origin. At some remote period they migrated southwestward along a route long afterward followed by the first white settlers of western Virginia and Carolina. With the high Appalachians as a center and stronghold, they spread over the adjoining lowlands in seven of our present states.

The original nucleus of the tribe, in the South, seems to have been the Kituhwa settlement, near the lower edge of what is now the Qualla boundary, adjoining the site of Bryson City, North Carolina. Their national capitol was Echota, just above the mouth of Tellico River, in southwestern Tennessee.

It was a quest for gold that first led white men into the Cherokee country, and nearly three centuries later it was another gold fever of the whites that wrought the Cherokees' undoing.

In 1540 the Spanish explorer, De Soto, came to an Indian town on the lower Savannah that was governed by a woman chief or "queen." Here he was shown implements of copper that appeared to be mixed with precious metal. These, he was told, came from a mountain province in the north.

De Soto seized the Indian queen as a prisoner and compelled her to go with him as a guide. She, however, led him astray over mazy courses and finally made her escape, leaving him

1

De Soto seized the Indian queen as a prisoner and compelled her to go with him as a guide.

She, however, led him astray over mazy courses and finally made her escape...

The Cherokee were successful farmers, growing a variety of crops that included corn, beans, and squash.

in a bare wilderness with his men and horses fairly worn out with hunger.

De Soto turned westward crossing "very rough and high ridges," to the upper waters of the French Broad, thence southerly until he reached some Cherokee settlements, where he was hospitably received. Still no gold was found, and the only treasure that he carried back was a dressed buffalo skin, the first ever seen by white men.

Long before their discovery by Europeans, the Cherokees had developed for themselves the rudiments of civilization. They were not roving hunters but dwelt in villages of log huts and cultivated the soil. They raised corn, beans, potatoes, (probably some variety of sweet potato), squashes and fruits; also practiced various simple industries. Their tribal organization, though looser than the confederacy of the Iroquois, was yet coherent enough for the whites to recognize as the "Cherokee Nation."

Scotch and Irish traders began to traffic with the Cherokees about the middle of the 17th century. Some of them remained and intermarried with the Indians, gaining much influence over them. Yet whatever tendency such mingling may have had toward bringing the Cherokees into friendly relations with the

British was neutralized by the haughty bearing and ruthless policy of the border settlers and provincial governments.

It is a commonplace of history that our own colonists, wherever they encountered Indians, stirred up bad blood and then proceeded to spill it. The French, for the most part only traders, and relatively few in number, were content to let the Indians live their own life in their own way. For this reason the French had little trouble with the natives. The English, on the contrary, came in swarms, with greed of land and a fixed purpose to seize and hold. So it resulted that when war broke out between the French and English (in America), most of the native tribes sided with the New France.

In this crisis the Cherokees found themselves in a pinch between conflicting interests. Their hearts really were with the French, but they were constrained to ally themselves with the English for protection against their hereditary foes, the neighboring Indian tribes, who had promptly gone over to the French side.

They were destined to rue the bargain, for they fell out with the English long before the war was over. They were attacked by them and overrun, half their warriors were killed, and the survivors were brought to such extremity by smallpox and starvation that they had to sue for peace on any terms. This involved, of course, large cessions of land.

In spite of this experience the Cherokees again joined sides with England when the struggle came between Colonies and Crown. Their reason was that American frontiersmen had already begun surging westward and taking everything they could hold by force of arms. Tennessee and Kentucky were partly occupied by them. The Cherokees found themselves almost surrounded by whites of a class that regarded red men simply as vermin to be exterminated. Against this encompassing death, England offered them protection.

In the summer of 1776, the Americans quickly mobilized their riflemen and struck at once, in overwhelming force, from four different

It is a commonplace of history that our own colonists, wherever they encountered Indians, stirred up bad blood and then proceeded to spill it.

directions. They destroyed nearly all the Cherokee towns, granaries, orchards, and growing crops; killed or drove off the cattle and horses; slaughtered all Indians who resisted; and scattered the wretched remainder into the wildest recesses of the mountains. Here there was no sustenance but roots, chestnuts, acorns, and such few animals as harbor in those dreary roughs.

It is not nice to recall, but it is naked truth, that our backwoodsmen, regarding the Indians as mere heathen and cumberers of the earth, displayed the same ferocity in fighting them as is shown by savages and by whites gone wild with fanaticism. They slew without regard for age or sex. They scalped the victims, and collected bounties for those scalps from their own governments. They did not consign captives to death by torture, after the Indian fashion, but they coolly murdered the feeble and carried away the strong to be sold into lifelong slavery.

In Col. William Christian's army of Virginians was a man named Ross, who left a journal of their expedition against the Cherokee towns in western Carolina. In describing a personal encounter during one of the battles, he said:—

"A stout Indian engaged a sturdy young white man who was a good bruiser and expert at gouging. After breaking their guns on each other they laid hold of one another; when the Cracker had his thumbs instantly in the fellow's eyes, who roared and cried *('canaly')*—enough, in English. 'Damn you,' says the white man, 'you can never have enough while you are alive.' He then threw him down, set his foot upon his head, and scalped him alive; then took up one of the broken guns and knocked out his brains. It would have been fun if he had let the latter action alone and sent him home without his nightcap to tell his countrymen how he had been treated."

That a white savage should do such a thing to a red savage is not so strange, but that a fairly educated man of some standing should be capable of such comment is hideously illuminating to those who seek true pictures of the 18th century border life.

Some of the Cherokees continued to fight the colonies until the close of the Revolution, but the main body succumbed after the first disaster and surrendered to the adjoining States a great part of their territory.

The first treaty with the new government of the United States was concluded in 1785. All of the Cherokee lands east of the Blue Ridge and much of the northern boundary, were ceded to the whites. But the ink was hardly dry on the parchment before there began a conflict between State and Federal authority as to the remaining Indian land. Intruders swarmed into it. The Indians protested in vain. Bloody forays and reprisals were followed by open war in 1792.

Six years later another peace treaty was concluded, with more

"A stout Indian engaged a sturdy young white man who was a good bruiser and expert at gouging.... when the Cracker had his thumbs instantly in the fellow's eyes, who roared and cried ('canaly') — enough, in English. 'Damn you,' says the white man, 'you can never have enough, while you are alive.'"

cessions of land, and with the usual guarantee on the part of the United States that thereafter the Cherokees should be left in possession of their country forever.

The retirement of the British to Canada, and the abandonment by Spain of claims east of the Mississippi, left both the northern and the southern tribes without any foreign backing; but the second war with Great Britain gave them a fresh opportunity. The Shawnee chief, Tecumseh, whose confederacy had been shattered at Tippecanoe, now rallied his forces and made common cause with England in the north. The Creeks in the south took to the warpath in 1813.

In this contest the Cherokees sided with the Americans. It was largely due to their help that General Andrew Jackson won a final victory over the Creeks at the Horseshoe Bend (Tohopeka), as a result of which most of the Creek territory passed over to the United States. How Jackson requited their aid will be seen in the sequel.

At the opening of the 19th century, the Cherokees had recovered from the ravages of war and were making rapid progress in the arts of peace. Their number had increased to about 20,000. Their fields and orchards were well cared for and prolific. Nearly every Indian had two or more horses, some of them owned cattle, and there was an abundance of hogs and poultry. The Federal government was encouraging indus-try by introducing plows and spinning wheels and looms.

There were some able men in the Nation, educated and quite as fit to lead or represent their people as the officers or politicians of the neighboring whites. Many were of mixed blood, descended in part from resident traders of the pre-Revolutionary period. These were not shiftless adventurers of "squaw-man" type but more like the Hudson Bay factors, men of good stock and character, who married regularly into the tribe and sent their children away to be educated or brought in private teachers from outside.

Such were the Daugherrys and the Adairs, the Rosses and the Woffords. Nancy Ward, a woman of great influence who was friendly to the Americans, was the daughter of a British officer by the sister of Atakullakulla, principal chief of the Cherokee Nation. General Samuel Houston, it may be remembered, took for his second wife the daughter of a Cherokee chief.

The Cherokee still remained in recognized possession of a region as large as Ohio, about half of it being within the present limits of Tennessee, and the rest in Georgia, Alabama, and the southwest corner of North Carolina. This is marked on the old maps "Cherokee Country" or "Cherokee Nation," the United States claiming no jurisdiction over it.

If the Indians had nothing but the Federal government to deal with they might perhaps have secured just treatment. President Jefferson acknowledged their title and sovereignty within the limits fixed by treaty. It was a region very desirable for the future expansion of the whites, and coveted by them, but to which they had neither legal nor moral right. It had been guaranteed to the Indians in perpetuity by the Government.

But our own Union in those days was loosely knit. The boundaries of those States bordering on the Cherokee country had been run without regard for Indian claims. Georgia, which then included all of what are now Alabama and Mississippi, claimed everything within its chartered limits, under the doctrine of State sovereignty, regardless of treaties negotiated by the Federal government.

Among the Cherokees themselves there was a disturbing element—a conservative, irreconcilable group that disdained civilization and dreamed of a free hunting ground far away where they should never be molested by the whites.

Taking advantage of this split between Indian factions, our Government then sought to compromise by proposing that the conservative Cherokees cede their proportionate share of land in return for a tract in the West, where they could enjoy the unfettered life of hunters and follow their primitive ancient ways. A treaty was negotiated, not with the Cherokee Nation but with a few chiefs of these malcontents, where-by considerable areas in Georgia and Tennessee were given in exchange for a western reservation, to which some of the Indians emigrated.

The main body of the Cherokees bitterly protested that this treaty had been effected by improper means and influences, without authority of their Nation, and could only be regarded as another move toward driving them from the land of their fathers. They pointed to the evidences of their own progress in civilization and begged that they be not forced to abandon this hard-won status and exiled to a wild land where stress of environment, and the hostility of native western tribes, would tend to make them revert to savagery.

Their pleas fell on deaf ears. Still another treaty was virtually thrust upon them by which they lost more than one-fourth of their territory, and this was declared to be a "final adjustment" of all claims and differences.

In the face of such discouragements, or perhaps stimulated by them, the Cherokee now made extraordinary efforts to win recognition as a civilized and independent people. In 1820, at the suggestion of Thomas Jefferson, they formed a republican government modeled after that of the United States, and seven years later they adopted a constitution.

This was an assumption of distinct nationality, and their sovereignty was recognized by the United States. They passed laws for the collection of taxes, for repairs on roads, for the support of schools, for the suppression of intemperance and polygamy, and for preventing the sale of lands to the whites without the consent of the national council.

And now occurred among these Indians, from within, an astounding development of culture which for originality and swiftness of accomplishment has no precedent nor parallel in the history of the human race.

There was a Cherokee of mixed blood named Sequoya (Se-quah-yah) who through an accident in hunting had become a cripple for life. Being unable to follow the chase, he took to sedentary occupations and developed considerable mechanical skill, especially in silver-working. He never learned to speak English, and of course could neither read nor write.

Sequoya had observed that the whites had a way of "talking on paper" whereby messages were sent and records were preserved. It set him to brooding over a project for devising a similar system for his own people. Being an old-fashioned Indian true to his own religion, he did not seek help from the missionaries, and they in turn discouraged him. But by himself he pondered long and earnestly over the mystery of the talking paper.

Like every other inventor of writing he began by trying to make a separate symbol for every word or idea. This proved an utterly hopeless scheme. In Cherokee there were thousands and tens of thousands of words. Even if so many symbols were designed, no man could remember half of them.

After years of hard study, in the face of ridicule and repeated failures, Sequoya finally began analyzing his language into its component sounds. He had no conception of vowels and consonants, but he picked out the distinct syllables of his mother tongue and found there

And now occurred among these Indians, from within, an astounding development of culture which for originality and swiftness of accomplishment has no precedent nor parallel in the history of the human race.

were only one hundred and fifteen.

Then came the brilliant solution of his problem; he would assign a separate character to each syllable, and any word in the Cherokee language could be written. For example, *kalanu* (raven) would be expressed by three symbols standing respectively for *ka*, *la*, and *nu*.

From an old spelling book he took the English alphabet and numerals, without the least idea of their sound or significance, and finding there were not enough characters for his purpose he devised others of his own. Most of the double consonants in Cherokee being formed with the hissing sound of *s*, he made a separate mark for it (when used as the initial of a syllable) and so reduced his syllabary to eighty-five characters. The mark for *s* and the one for the nasal *u* (like the un in hung) are the only actual letters in his system, as the vowel characters are used only when they form separate syllables.

The effect of this invention was amazing. Any one who could speak Cherokee, having once learned the sight and sound of these eighty-five marks, could at once read and write the language with precision. There was no arbitrary spelling to learn. Any Indian could pick up in a few weeks what it takes our own children at least two years of hard work to acquire. A bright child or adult could master the art of reading and writing in a few days.

As if by magic the education of the Cherokees became an accomplished fact. Through this invention of an illiterate, thousands of them became literate, without one school being established or one teacher hired.

Although Sequoya himself was a pagan, and remained so to the end of his days, the first literary fruit of his writing system was a translation of a part of St. John's gospel, made by a native convert.

In 1827, the Cherokee Council resolved to establish a national newspaper in their own language. Types for that purpose were cast in Boston. The press, types, and paper were laboriously transported to the capital at New Echota. The type cases and other furniture were made on the spot, an office was set up in a log hut and thus began publication of the *Cherokee Phoenix*, under the editorship of Elias Boudinot, a young Indian who had been educated in Connecticut by the American Board of Commissioners for Foreign Missions.

Meantime the formation by the Cherokees of a national government caused a rupture between the Federal and State authorities. President Monroe approved the suggestion of the Indian agent that the Cherokee lands be allotted, the surplus sold for their benefit, and the Indians invested with full rights of citizenship in the States where they resided. But Tennessee, North Carolina, and Georgia refused to allow any Indians to live within their boundaries on any pretext whatever. Georgia further demanded cession of all Indian lands within the limits of her charter.

Sequoya never learned to speak or write in English,
but he invented the written form of the Cherokee language.

Cherokee Alphabet

D a	**R** e	**T** i	**Ꮼ** o	**O** u	**i** v	
S ga **Ꮼ** ka	**Ᏺ** ge	**Ᏽ** gi	**A** go	**J** gu	**E** gv	
Ꮟ ha	**Ᏸ** he	**Ꮀ** hi	**Ᏺ** ho	**Γ** hu	**Ꭴ** hv	
W la	**Ꮢ** le	**Ꮅ** li	**G** lo	**M** lu	**Ꭹ** lv	
Ꮊ ma	**Ꮎ** me	**H** mi	**Ꮽ** mo	**Ꮉ** mu		
Ꮎ na **Ꮏ** hna **G** nah	**Ꮑ** ne	**Ꮒ** ni	**Z** no	**Ꮔ** nu	**O** nv	
Ꮖ qua	**Ꮙ** que	**Ᏼ** qui	**Ꮗ** quo	**Ꮘ** quu	**Ꮛ** quv	
Ꮂ sa **Ꮿ** s	**Ꮴ** se	**Ꮾ** si	**Ꮼ** so	**Ꮡ** su	**R** sv	
Ꮣ da **Ꮤ** ta	**Ꮥ** de **Ꮦ** te	**Ꮧ** di **Ꮨ** ti	**V** do	**S** du	**Ꮩ** dv	
Ꮬ dla **Ꮯ** tla	**Ꮮ** tle	**C** tli	**Ꮶ** tlo	**Ꮰ** tlu	**P** tlv	
Ꮳ tsa	**Ꮴ** tse	**Ꮧ** tsi	**K** tso	**Ꮫ** tsa	**C** tsv	
Ꮹ wa	**Ꮺ** we	**Ꮼ** wi	**Ꮿ** wo	**Ꮎ** wu	**6** wv	
Ꮿ ya	**Ᏸ** ye	**Ꮏ** yi	**Ꮙ** yo	**G** yu	**B** yu	

Sounds represented by vowels
a, as a in father, or short as a in rival
e, as a in hate, or short as e in met
i, as i in pig, or short as i in pit
o, as o in note, approaching aw in law
u, as oo in fool, or short as u in pull
v, as u in but, nasalized

Consonant sounds
g, nearly as in English, but approaching to k
d, nearly as in English, but approaching to t
h, k, l, m, n, q, s, t, w, y, as in English
Syllables beginning with g except **S** (ga) sometimes have the power of k.
V (do) **S** (du) **Ꮩ** (dv) sometimes sound to, tu, tv.
Syllables written with tl except **C** (tla) sometimes vary to dl.

Elias Boudinet became the first editor of the Cherokee Phoenix, a newspaper published in the newly created written Cherokee language.

Naturally the Cherokees protested that their limits were defined by treaties with the United States, and they declared that "It is the fixed and unalterable determination of this Nation never again to cede one foot more of land."

The Governor of Georgia in reply blamed the missionaries for the refusal of the Indians to "move on" and informed the Federal government that if it backed up the Indians and resisted occupancy of their lands by Georgians it would have a fratricidal war on its hands.

The thread of Indian tenure thus strained was soon snapped by an unexpected turn of affairs. Gold was discovered in the Cherokee country, and the white man's greed burst all bonds of law or morality. At the same time Andrew Jackson, an out-and-out Indian hater, became President of the United States. From that moment the doom of the Cherokees was sealed.

How the Cherokee Nation was then driven at the point of the bayonet to the far West, and by what strange means a few hundred of their people, starving in the gulfs of the Great Smoky Mountains, but still indomitable, were at last permitted to retain a fragment of their ancient birthright, is one of the most dramatic episodes in American history.

The existence of gold in the Cherokee country was well known to Spanish adventurers who followed after De Soto in the last half of the sixteenth century. There is evidence that they carried on some mining operations in that region. But they kept their knowledge secret, and it perished when they left the country. Then a century went by before the English appeared on the scene, and another century before any gold finds were reported in the South.

In North Carolina the first mint returns appeared in 1793. Six years later a 17-pound nugget was discovered on the Reed plantation in Cabarrus County, and in 1823 one was found that weighed 28 pounds. Here and in adjoining districts the placer ground was vigorously worked, and much nugget gold was taken out.

From 1804 to 1827, all the gold produced in the United States came from North Carolina. It was from the Piedmont region, east of the mountains, and not within the Cherokee country.

In 1828, gold was discovered in the mountains of Burke County, North Carolina, and the auriferous belt was at once traced southward along the edge of the Indian territory. About the same time some of the precious metal was found near the present Dahlonega, within the boundary of the Cherokee Nation, but in the part claimed by Georgia. Then the Georgians went wild.

"...intrusive mining ceased then and there, and swindling mining commenced."

In December, 1828, one month after Andrew Jackson's election to the presidency of the United States, the Georgia legislature passed an act annexing that part of the Cherokee country within her chartered limits. It was further ordained that after the first day of June, 1830, all laws, usages and customs of the Cherokee Indians should be null and void within that region; that all Indians remaining within it should be subject to such laws as Georgia might enact; and that no Indian, or descendent of an Indian, should be deemed a competent witness or a party to any suit in any court where a white man was a defendant.

The confiscated territory was then mapped out by state surveyors into "land lots" of 160 acres each, and "gold lots" of 40 acres, which were put up at public lottery, each white citizen of Georgia being given a ticket.

A caustic but truthful writer of the time remarked that "intrusive mining ceased then and there, and swindling mining commenced." So far as gold was concerned, most of the supposed mineral veins proved to be barren; but the land lottery was a different matter.

By laws passed later, every Cherokee head of a family was nominally

The land of the Cherokees once stretched from South Carolina to northern Kentucky. Today the Qualla Reservation, populated by the eastern band, encompasses 56,000 square acres.

granted an allotment of 160 acres. This was a barren gift as other laws enacted made it impossible for the Indian owner to defend his right in any court, or to prevent the seizure of his homestead, or even of his own dwelling house, by any white who saw fit to oust him. If he resisted he was subject to imprisonment.

Any contract between a white man and an Indian was declared invalid unless established by the testimony of two white witnesses. This virtually cancelled all debts due from white men to Indians. An Indian was forbidden to dig for gold on his own land. Armed bands of Georgians now swept over the country, seizing or destroying Indian property and assaulting any of the owners who resisted.

There were among the Cherokees some white teachers, missionaries and printers, who had been sent there by permission of the President of the United States. In order to get rid of them, or at least shut their mouths about the spoliation, Georgia demanded that they take a special oath of allegiance to the State. Those who refused were sent to the penitentiary.

In 1832, the Supreme Court of the United States, of which John Marshall was Chief-justice, decided that the Cherokees formed a distinct community in which the laws of Georgia had no force, declared the act of Georgia in seizing their lands to be void, and ordered the release of the missionaries.

With regard to Georgia's claim that the land in question was within her chartered limits, the Supreme Court ruled that a charter granted by the King of Great Britain to one of her colonies merely regulated the rights of the discoverers among themselves, but could not affect the rights of those already in possession as aboriginal occupants. It simply conferred the exclusive right of purchasing such lands as the natives were willing to sell. The treaties with the Cherokees bound them as a dependent ally of the United States claiming and receiving the protection of a powerful friend and neighbor, but without involving a surrender of their national character.

It is said that when the action of the court was announced, President Jackson remarked, "John Marshall has made his decision, now let him enforce it." The Governor of Georgia had defied the summons, with threat of rebellion. He now ignored the Supreme Court's decision and kept the imprisoned missionaries at hard labor among felons for more than a year.

The Cherokees were staring ruin in the face. As a last resort they submitted to Washington a memorial proposing to satisfy Georgia by ceding to her a part of their lands, they to be protected in possession of the remainder for a definite period to be fixed by the United States, after which, having disposed of their surplus lands, they should become citizens of the various States within which they resided.

Their plea might as well have been addressed to the North Star. Bluntly they were told that the only way out of their troubles was for them to give up the land of their fathers and emigrate in a body to the far West.

It would be to the honor of the Government if then and there an end had been made to subterfuge and the bayonets of the ejectors frankly bared. No doubt that would have been Jackson's way if he had been dictator. But some pretext of bargaining with the Indians had to be found to give color of legality to their banishment. And now a sly politician, in the garb of a Christian minister, steps into the plot.

Among the Cherokees there was a small faction that favored the idea of emigrating. With the leaders of this faction a commissioner, in the person of Reverend J. F. Schermerhorn, drew up the terms of a treaty binding the Cherokee Nation to surrender their whole territory and move west, in consideration of a sum of money and a new territory beyond the Mississippi. The deal, however, could not be concluded until ratified by the Nation in full council assembled. Schermerhorn then visited the Cherokee country and tried for six months to induce the national council to approve this treaty; but he completely failed. The reverend emissary then suggested to the Secretary of War two alternative propositions: (1) to get the signatures of influential Cherokees by buying up their personal improvements at their own valuation, if any degree reasonable; or (2) to make a treaty with a part of the Cherokees and compel the rest to accept it.

Jackson, although ruthless himself in dealing with the Indians, could not stomach this. He replied pointedly that the treaty, if concluded at all, must be procured on fair and open terms, with no special inducement to any individual, high or low, to win his aid or influence, and without sacrificing the interest of the whole to the cupidity of a few.

In October, 1835, the national council of the Cherokees, led by their great chief John Ross, unanimously rejected the treaty framed by Schermerhorn, even the original signers repudiating it. The commissioner concealed his chagrin by reporting, "I have pressed Ross so hard by the course I have adopted that although he got the general council to pass a resolution declaring that they would not treat on the basis of the five million dollars, yet he has been forced to bring the Nation to agree to a treaty, here or in Washington. They have used every effort to get by me and get to Washington again this winter. They dare not yet do it."

He explained the defection of the minority leaders by intimating that they feared for their personal safety. "But," he piously added; "the Lord is able to overrule all things for good."

The reason for heading the Indians away from Washington was that

Ross was a man of such high character, ability, and impressive personality that his influence was feared if he could get in touch with Congress, and there was already a powerful opposition to the administration's Indian policy.

At the October meeting of the council, notice was served on the Cherokee Nation to meet Schermerhorn and the Governor of Tennessee, as commissioners, at New Echota in the following December, for the purpose of negotiating a treaty, and it was declared that all who failed to attend would be counted as assenting to whatever treaty might be made.

But these commissioners were not empowered to deal on any other basis than the one that the Cherokees had already rejected. Therefore Ross determined to carry their case direct to Washington. He had moved his home to Tennessee, to escape persecution by the Georgia authorities; but they, hearing of his intended visit to Washington, sent a body of Georgia militia across the line into Tennessee, arrested Ross, confiscated all his private papers and the proceedings of the council, and carried him into Georgia, where he was held for a time without charge.

The poet, John Howard Payne, author of *Home, Sweet, Home*, was stopping with Ross at the time, collecting scientific data relating to the Indians. He likewise was seized, and his manuscripts taken from him. At the same time the national newspaper, The *Cherokee Phoenix*, was suppressed.

John Ross, the chief of the national council of Cherokees, was arrested by Georgia's militia before he could take his case for the Cherokee people to Washington.

By such acts as these, in plain defiance of the law of the land. the Cherokees, at the most critical time in their history, were deprived of their teacher, their national press, and the one spokesman whose voice at the seat of government might have won them a hearing.

When the time came for the assembling at New Echota, not over 300 Cherokees, men, women, and children, were present, out of a population of over 17,000. The Governor of Tennessee was absent. Schermerhorn, on the one side, and a dozen Indians as committeemen, on the other, negotiated a treaty that sealed the doom of the whole Cherokee Nation.

This instrument provided that the Cherokees cede to the United States all of their remaining territory east of the Mississippi for the sum of five million dollars and a common joint interest in the region already occupied by those Cherokees who had gone west at an earlier date. This region was situated within what are now Oklahoma and Kansas. Improvements on the eastern lands were to be paid for, and the Indians removed at the expense of the Government and subsisted for one year after their arrival in the West.

Soon after this farce had been enacted, the War Department sent into the Cherokee country a confidential agent, Major W. M. Davis. He reported as follows:—

"Sir, that paper,... called a treaty, is no treaty at all, because not sanctioned by the great body of the Cherokees, and made without their participation or assent. I solemnly declare to you that upon its reference to the Cherokee people it would be instantly rejected by nine-tenths of them and I believe by nineteen-twentieths of them. There were not present at the conclusion of the treaty more than one hundred Cherokee voters....The most cunning and artful means were resorted to to conceal the paucity of numbers present at the treaty. No enumeration of them was made by Schermerhorn. The business of making the treaty was transacted with a committee, appointed by the Indians present, so as not to expose their numbers. The power of attorney under which the committee acted was signed only by the president and secretary of the meeting, so as not to disclose their weakness.... Mr. Schermerhorn's apparent design was to conceal the real number present and to impose upon the public and the Government upon this point.... I now warn you and the President that if this paper of Schermerhorn's called a treaty is sent to the Senate and ratified you will bring trouble upon the Government and eventually destroy the Cherokee Nation. The Cherokees are a peaceable, harmless people, but you may drive them to desperation, and this treaty cannot be carried into effect except by the strong arm of force."

Chief Ross and a body of national delegates sent protests to Washing-

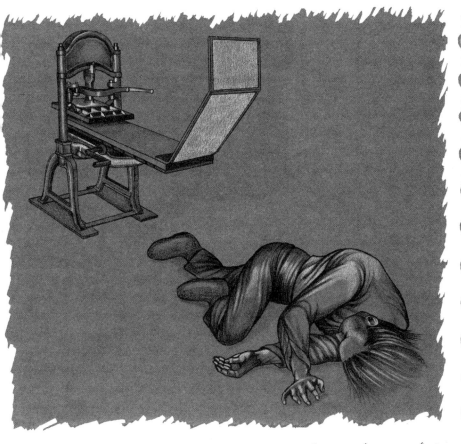

By such acts as these, in plain defiance of the
law of the land, the Cherokees, at the most
critical time in their history,
were deprived of their teacher, their
national press, and the one spokesman
whose voice at the seat of government
might have won them a hearing.

ton with signatures representing nearly 16,000 Cherokees. Resolutions denouncing the treaty were presented to General Wool, commanding United States troops who had been sent into the Cherokee country "to look down opposition," and he forwarded them to Washington. The General received for his pains a stinging reprimand from President Jackson, who declared that no communication whatever would be held with Ross, and that no council would be permitted even to discuss the treaty.

The outrageous injustice suffered by the Cherokees, without one retaliatory act on their part, excited the sympathy of decent people everywhere. And yet the "treaty," so infamously concocted and so brazenly sustained by the administration, passed the Senate by the margin of one vote, and was proclaimed by the President on the 23rd of May, 1836. The Indians were given two years from this date in which to abandon the land of their fathers and move a thousand miles to the western wilderness.

Some of the ablest leaders in Congress, northern and southern, were bitterly opposed to the treaty. It was denounced by Daniel Webster, Edward Everett, Henry Wise and Henry Clay. A few years earlier Jackson's Indian policy had been scathingly rebuked by sturdy old Davy Crockett, who cried shame upon it as unjust, dishonest, cruel and shortsighted. "I had considered a treaty," said he, "as a sovereign law of the land, and now I hear it considered as a matter of expedience."

Crockett's own constituents were immediately interested in the removal of the Indians. He had been elected to Congress from Tennessee as a Jacksonian Democrat, and he had been threatened that if he did not advocate the forcible removal of the Cherokees his public career would be summarily cut off; but he declared on the floor of the House that he could not permit himself to please his constituents and his colleagues at the expense of his honor and his conscience. Jackson never forgave him; and the threat to eject Crockett from politics was carried out.

False reports were now circulated that Chief Ross and other leaders were seeking to excite the Cherokees to war, and the militia of the surrounding states were put in the field to prevent or suppress it. General R. E. Dunlap, commanding the East Tennessee volunteers, found on the contrary that it was the Indians, and not the whites, that needed protection. In a speech to his brigade at their disbandment he said:—

"My course has excited the hatred of a few of the lawless rabble in Georgia, who have long played the part of unfeeling petty tyrants, and that to the disgrace of the proud character of gallant soldiers and good citizens. I had determined that I would never dishonor the Tennessee arms in a servile service by aiding to carry into execution at the point of the bayonet a treaty made by a lean minority against the will and authority of the Cherokee People.... I soon discovered that the Indians had not the most distant thought of war with the United States, notwithstanding the common rights of humanity and justice had been denied them."

General Wool was ordered to disarm the Cherokees and overawe them by a display of force. While going about this work he was manifestly disgusted with the role and sick at heart. In one of his letters he declared:—

"If I could (and I could not do them a greater kindness) I would remove every Indian tomorrow beyond the reach of the white men, who, like vultures, are watching, ready to pounce upon their prey and strip them of everything they have or expect from the Government of the United States. Yes, sir, nineteen-twentieths, if not ninety-nine out of every hundred, will go penniless to the West."

Nemesis fell heavily upon the very men who signed the treaty at New Echota as Indian committeemen. Their leader, Major John Ridge, who had negotiated the first treaty with Schermerhom, was obliged to appeal to President Jackson for protection against the harpies who beset him and his neighbors:—

"They have got our lands and now they are preparing to fleece us of the money accruing from the treaty. We found our plantations taken either in whole or in part by the Georgians—suits instituted against us for back rents for our farms. These suits are commenced in the inferior courts, with the evident design that, when we are ready to remove, to arrest our people, and on these vile claims to induce us to compromise for our own release, to travel with our families. Thus our funds will be filched from our people, and we shall be compelled to leave our country as beggars and in want.

"Even the Georgia laws, which deny us our oaths, are thrown aside. ...The lowest classes of the white people are flogging the Cherokees with cowhides, hickories and clubs. We are not safe in our houses—our people are assailed by day and night by the rabble. Even justices of the peace and constables are concerned in this business. This barbarous treatment is not confined to men, but women are stripped also and whipped without law or mercy.... Send regular troops to protect us.... If it is not done we shall carry off nothing but the scars of the lash upon our backs, and our oppressors will get all the money. We talk plainly, as chiefs having property and life in danger."

A few of the Indians accepted outfits and moved voluntarily to the West, but the main body sternly refused to go. It took all of Ross's influence to preserve the peace, and military officers on the spot reported that he alone stood between the whites and bloodshed. In February,

1837, General Wool called the Cherokees together and made them a speech counciling prudence and submission to the inevitable. The result he reported to the Adjutant-General at Washington:—

"It is, however, vain to talk to a people almost universally opposed to the treaty and who maintain that they never made such a treaty. So determined are they in their opposition that not one of all those who were present and voted at the council held but a day or two since, however poor and destitute, would receive either rations or clothing from the United States lest they might compromise themselves in regard to the treaty. These same people, as well as those in the mountains of North Carolina, during the past summer preferred living upon the roots and sap of trees rather than receive provisions from the United States, and thousands, as I have been informed, had no other food for weeks."

Soon after making this report, General Wool was relieved from command at his own request.

Meantime Jackson had been succeeded in the presidency by Martin Van Buren. Word having reached Washington that the mass of the Cherokees did not intend to move to the West, Van Buren ordered General Winfield Scott to assume command of the troops already in the Cherokee country and to add to them a regiment of infantry, a regiment of artillery, and six companies of dragoons. Scott

Major John Ridge was the leader of the Indian committemen who doomed the entire Cherokee nation.

was further authorized, at his discretion, to call upon the governors of the four neighboring states for militia and volunteers, not exceeding four thousand in number, to aid in moving the Indians.

But public feeling was now so deeply stirred in sympathy with the Indians that Van Buren sought a compromise by proposing to allow them two years further time in which to move. To this suggestion Governor Gilmer, of Georgia, responded:

"It is necessary that I should know whether the President intends by the instruction to General Scott to require that the Indians shall be maintained in their occupancy by an armed force in opposition to the rights of the owners of the soil. If such be the intention, a direct collision between the authorities of the State and the General Government must ensue. My duty will require that I shall prevent any interference whatever by the troops with the rights of the State and its citizens. I shall not fail to perform it."

Van Buren hastily explained that no such action was contemplated, and he proceeded to carry out the original schedule.

On the 10th of May, 1838, General Scott issued a proclamation to the Cherokees in which he announced that:—

"The President of the United States has sent me with a powerful army to cause you, in obedience to the treaty of 1835, to join that part of your people who are already established in prosperity on the other side of the Mississippi. Unhappily the two years…allowed for that purpose you have suffered to pass away…without making any preparation to follow, and now…the emigration must be commenced in haste….The full moon of May is already on the wane, and before another shall have passed away every Cherokee, man, woman, and child…must be in motion to join their brethren in the far West….I have come to carry out that determination. My troops already occupy many positions…and thousands and thousands are approaching from every quarter to render resistance and escape alike hopeless….Will you then by resistance compel us to resort to arms?…Or will you by flight seek to hide yourselves in mountains and forests and thus oblige us to hunt you down? Remember that in pursuit it may be impossible to avoid conflicts. The blood of the white man or the blood of the red man may be spilt, and if spilt, however accidentally, it may be impossible for the discreet and humane among us, to prevent a general war and carnage."

Let us now briefly summarize the situation:—

The Cherokees of the South, by a census taken in 1835, numbered 16,542, exclusive of 1,592 negro slaves, and 201 whites intermarried with the Indians. They were entirely self-supporting. They grew bountiful crops of corn, wheat, oats, cotton, potatoes, indigo and tobacco. Their apple and peach orchards were prolific. Much attention was given to gardening. They had plenty of cattle, horses, sheep, goats and swine. Many families made butter and cheese.

Cotton and woolen cloths and blankets were manufactured by the women. Considerable trade was carried on with the neighboring States. In boats of their own, the Cherokees exported much cotton to New Orleans. The Nation had no debt, and the revenue was sufficient for public purposes. The roads were in good condition, and at convenient distances along the routes, inns were kept by natives.

Nearly all Cherokees could read and write their own language. Schools were increasing every year. There was a national press (or had been until the Georgians destroyed it). Some of the leading men of the Nation were highly educated according to the standard of the time, and could hold their own in discussion with statesmen anywhere.

The Cherokees were the mountaineers of the South. Like all highlanders, of whatever race, they were passionately attached to the rugged but healthful and picturesque land that gave them birth. The promise of a far away wilderness, encompassed and disputed by savages, in exchange for their ancient villages and cultivated fields, held no allurements for a people that was prosper-

ous in the arts of peace and asked nothing better than to be let alone.

They had been at peace with the United States for forty years. The last war in which they had been engaged was when they fought shoulder to shoulder with the Americans against the Indian allies of Great Britain. If it had not been for their charge against the enemy's rear at the battle of the Horseshoe Bend it is probable that General Jackson would have been obliged to retire, instead of winning that decisive victory.

The nationality of the Cherokees, and their clear title to the soil they occupied, had been confirmed by the Supreme Court, which ruled that the sea-to-sea charters of the British gave the States that had succeeded to them merely exclusive rights to buy land from the Indians, but no right to force such sales. The territory of the Cherokees was separated from that of any other state within whose chartered limits they might reside by a boundary line established by treaties, and within that boundary the Indians possessed rights with which no State could interfere. The Federal Government had guaranteed the Cherokees by treaty that their territory should remain inviolate forever.

And yet President Jackson, with a frontiersman's contempt for Indians, and an arrogance that brooked no opposition from any quarter, disputed the ruling of the Supreme Court and forthwith proceeded to violate it. His weak-kneed successor, seeking to temporize, was shaken back into direct action by the threatening hand of a State executive. And now came a force of 7,000 troops, with artillery, to round up and drive out the Cherokees, who if they had wanted to fight and had possessed arms with which to fight, could not have mustered more than half as many men, to say nothing of the myriads that were at the call of the President if reinforcements for Scott's army had been needed.

One can feel today the sting in the words of old chief Junaluska; "If I had known that Jackson would drive us from our homes, I would have killed him that day at the Horseshoe."

The Cherokees preserved to the end an unwavering devotion to their great chief Ross and a pathetic trust in his ability to persuade Congress to let them remain in their old home. He did all that a wise and brave leader could do to preserve the peace and rescue for his people at least a moiety of what was by right and in honor due them.

On the advice of Ross, the Indians had given up their arms to General Wool, so that no suspicion of ill intent could be harbored against them. They did this even though it left them defenseless against the rabble who harried and robbed them behind the backs of the Federal troops.

Despite repeated rebuffs at Washington, and threats against his person and property at home, Ross once more sent to Congress a protest and memorial in the name of the Cherokee Nation. This was delivered in March, 1838. At the same time a memorial from citizens of New York was submitted calling for an inquiry into the validity of the treaty of 1835. The ensuing debate in both houses of Congress was "characterized by a depth and bitterness of feeling such as had never been exceeded even on the slavery question." Henry A. Wise, who was a member of the House of Representatives from Virginia, declared "without fear of contradiction" that there was not one man in that House or out of it, who had read the proceedings of the case, who would say that there had ever been any assent given to that treaty by the Cherokee Nation." In replying to Mr. Halsey of Georgia he told him that an ex-governor of Halsey's own

> *"If I had known that Jackson would drive us from our homes, I would have killed him that day at the Horseshoe."*
>
> — *Chief Junaluska*

State, who had declared that Georgia must and would have the Cherokee lands, would not gain greatly by comparison, either in civilization or morals, with the Cherokee chief, John Ross.

This chief Ross, by the way, was only one-eighth of Indian blood. His father and maternal grandfather were born in Scotland, and his mother was only a quarter-blood Cherokee. From 1809 until his death, in 1866, he was in the constant service of his people. He was adjutant of the Cherokee regiment that turned the tide of battle for General Jackson at the Horseshoe Bend. He was a member, and then president, of the national committee of the Cherokee council.

In 1827, he was president of the convention that framed and adopted the constitution of the Cherokee Nation, "the first effort at a regular government, with distinct branches and powers defined, ever made and carried into effect by any of the Indians of North America." In the following year he was elected principal chief of the Cherokee Nation, and he held this office continuously until his death.

After a hard fight in Congress both the Ross memorial and the one from New York were tabled. In May, President Van Buren made his belated proffer of a stay of proceedings, but then immediately backed down before the bristling Governor of Georgia. John Ross then submitted another project for the negotiation of a new treaty as a substitute for that of 1835, but the last day of grace for the voluntary emigration of the Cherokees was only one day off, and the Government declared that it could not consider any further negotiations.

Meantime General Scott had built a number of stockade forts throughout the Cherokee country and had disposed his troops in them. There were six of these forts in southwestern North Carolina, five in northern Georgia, one in northern Alabama, and one in southeastern Tennessee. When the last hour had struck he began the round-up.

There seems to be only one reliable and full account of the Cherokee removal. It is by Mr. James Mooney, of the United States Bureau of Ethnology, who was a master of the Cherokee language and a competent historian. The facts were collected by him directly from men, white and red, who were themselves participants in this tragic affair. A few paragraphs from Mr. Mooney's narrative are as follows:—

"Squads of troops were sent to search out with rifle and bayonet every small cabin hidden away in coves or by the sides of mountain streams, to seize and bring in as prisoners all the occupants, however or wherever they might be found. Families at dinner were startled by the sudden gleam of bayonets in the doorway, and rose up to be driven with blows and oaths along the weary miles of trail that led to the stockade.

"Men were seized in their fields or going along the road, women were taken from their wheels and children from their play. In many cases, in turning for one last look as they crossed the ridge, they saw their homes in flames, fired by the lawless rabble that followed on the heels of the soldiers to loot and pillage. So keen were these outlaws on the scent that in some instances they were driving off the cattle and other stock of the Indians almost before the soldiers had fairly started their owners in the other direction."

"Systematic hunts were made by the same men for Indian graves, to rob them of the silver pendants and other valuables deposited with the dead. A Georgian volunteer; afterward a colonel in the Confederate service said, 'I fought through the Civil War and have seen men shot to pieces and slaughtered by thousands, but the Cherokee removal was the cruelest work I ever knew.'"

In this manner, within a few weeks, nearly 17,000 of the Indians were corralled in the various stockades. The rest, about a thousand, mostly natives of the high mountains of southwestern North Carolina, fled and hid out in the trackless wilds of the Great Smoky divide.

Early in June the work of removal began. Several parties, aggregating about 5,000, were dispatched under direction of officers of the Army to landings on the Tennessee River, where they were put aboard steam-boats, sent down the Tennessee and the Ohio, to the further bank of the Mississippi, and then marched afoot across Arkansas to the recently established Indian Territory (now Oklahoma).

This removal, in the hottest part of the year, of a mountain-bred people unaccustomed to the scorching low-lands, unused to the kind of food given them, nauseated by the warm drinking water, and crowded together like sheep on the steamboats, was attended by much sickness and mortality. The Cherokee national council pleaded that they be allowed to remove the

"I fought through the Civil War and have seen men shot to pieces and slaughtered by thousands, but the Cherokee removal was the cruelest work I ever knew."

rest of their people overland, in parties led by their own chiefs, after the summer heat and sickly season had passed. This was permitted, and the remaining 13,000 started on their long trek, from their assembly place at Rattlesnake Springs, Tennessee, in October, 1838.

"It was like the march of an army, regiment after regiment, the wagons in the center, the officers along the line, and the horsemen on the flanks and at the rear.... The route lay south of Pikeville, through McMinnville and on to Nashville, where the Cumberland was crossed. Then they went on to Hopkinsville, Kentucky, where the noted chief White-path, in charge of a detachment, sickened and died. His people buried him by the roadside, with a box over the grave and poles with streamers around it, that the others coming on behind might note the spot and remember him."

"Somewhere also along that march of death—for the exiles died by tens and twenties every day of the journey—the devoted wife of John Ross sank down, leaving him to go on with the bitter pain of bereavement added to heartbreak at the ruin of his nation. The Ohio was crossed at a ferry near the mouth of the Cumberland, and the army passed on through southern Illinois until the great Mississippi was reached opposite Cape Girardeau, Missouri."

"It was now the middle of winter, with the river running full of ice, so that several detachments were obliged to wait some time on the eastern bank for the channel to become clear. In talking with old men and women at Tahlequah (Mr. Mooney) found that the lapse of over half a century had not sufficed to wipe out the memory of the miseries of that halt beside the frozen river, with hundreds of sick and dying penned up in wagons or stretched upon the ground, with only a blanket overhead to keep out the January blast."

At last the crossing was made, and the sad procession passed on through southern Missouri. In March, 1839, they reached their destination in Indian Territory, after nearly six months' travel and agonizing hardships. It is estimated that over 4,000 Cherokees perished as a direct result of the removal, or nearly one-fourth of all those who were driven into exile. A war with an enemy of anything like their own number would not have taken so heavy a toll.

The struggles and trials of the Cherokees in their new western home do not concern the present topic. Let us go back now to the scattered and desperate refugees, those pitiful few hundreds who were left outlawed in the forests of their native mountains.

It has already been mentioned that the original nucleus of the Cherokees was the Kituwha settlement on the Tuckaseegee River, near the mouth of the Okona-lufty,

"Men were seized in their fields or going along the road, women were taken from their wheels and children from their play.

In many cases, in turning for one last look as they crossed the ridge, they saw their homes in flame..."

in the present Swain County. North Carolina. The Indians of this and the neighboring settlements on Lufty and Soco were the purest blooded and most conservative of the Cherokee Nation. Their chief, Yonaguska ("Drowning Bear"), was a man of fine presence, six feet three inches in height and of powerful build. He was a noted orator. His people revered him not only as a leader but as a prophet.

Yonaguska counseled peace and friendship with the white man, but he was immovably opposed to a western migration. He declared that his people were safer from aggression in their steep and rocky mountains than they would ever be in a fertile land that would sooner or later be coveted by the westward-moving whites. He was a firm upholder of ancient customs and of the aboriginal religion. The white missionaries he regarded with suspicion.

When a Cherokee translation of St. Matthew was published at New Echota, and a copy was brought to the Kituwha country, Yonaguska would not allow it to be circulated until it had first been read to him-

"Well, it seems to be a good book — strange that the white people are no better, after having had it so long."

self. After listening to a few chapters the old chief dryly remarked; "Well, it seems to be a good book— strange that the white people are no better, after having had it so long."

When Scott's soldiers began to seize the Indians and drive them to the stockades, most of Yonaguska's band fled in advance and secreted themselves in the high mountains. Here they were joined by others who had escaped from Calhoun and other collecting stations, until upwards of a thousand Indians were hiding in the roughs. About half of them were under command of a leader named Utsala ("Lichen"), who disposed them along the head waters between Clingman Dome and Mount Guyot of the Great Smoky range.

Anyone acquainted with that region and knowing whites and Indians descended from those who were there at the time of the man-hunt, can visualize the situation in which the fugitives were placed.

Although lumbermen at one time began to invade it, it remains a wild country. Nearly all of it is very rough and rugged. Most of the divide (which forms the State line between

North Carolina and Tennessee) is over 5,500 feet above sea level, and the abutting ridges for several miles each way are but little lower. The sides of the mountains have steep slopes that begin at the very banks of the streams.

There are extensive areas strewn with great fragments of rock, although there is a heavy forest mantle everywhere. Cliffs and precipitous banks are so frequent that the only thoroughfares are a few carefully chosen trails. For several miles east of the Porter Gap the crest of the Smoky divide is almost knife-edged; so that footing is precarious, the rocks being covered with slippery moss or by dense, low, iron-like bushes that are very hard for a man to push through. A misstep might send one hurtling and sliding five hundred feet or more into North Carolina on one side or Tennessee on the other, unless some tree-top caught and held him.

On the slopes of the mountains there is a heavy stand of hardwood and chestnut and hemlock; on the upper reaches there is dense spruce and balsam. Labyrinths of laurel keep many of the water-courses in perpetual gloom. On some slopes and ridges, particularly on the Tennessee side, are great tracts of stunted rhododendron over which a man can only flounder. Dogs cannot go through such a thicket at all.

So far, then, as configuration and natural cover are concerned, this region is almost ideal for men hiding out, and to this day it is a refuge for moonshiners, deserters, and outlaws. But the problem of getting food in such a country is serious, unless the fugitive has clandestine help from outside.

There is little animal life in the upper zones, other than small brook trout, chipmunks, red squirrels, and a few birds. Bears harbor there, but they are wily and almost impossible to find without a pack of dogs. Formerly there were deer, and at that time a small party of hunters might be able to feed themselves for a week or two on products of the chase. But when a thousand fugitive Indians swarmed up into the roughs of the mountains, all game animals must have fled before them, leaving an empty solitude.

It was summer time; so there were no nuts nor acorns. Edible roots are seldom to be found in such a high land. There was little sustenance but toads, snakes, insects, berries, and the inner bark of trees. Many of the Indians starved to death. And yet the survivors stayed on, defying every effort of the troops to capture them.

General Scott found himself confronted by a problem similar, on a small scale, to the one that was giving so much trouble to our army operating against the Seminoles in the Everglades of Florida. To dig the Cherokees out of their warrens would require a large force operating simultaneously from both the Tennessee and the Carolina sides;

and beating through a country so difficult that the "drive" might last all summer. At this juncture there occurred an incident that gave him an opportunity for compromise.

Among the Indians who had been seized was an old man named Tsali (Cherokee pronunciation of Charley). He was taken with his wife, his brother, his three sons and their families. His wife being unable to travel fast, the soldiers prodded her along with bayonets. Charley, boiling with rage at this brutality, gave the word to the other men, in Cherokee, to strike down the guard and make a dash for liberty. They sprang upon the unsuspecting soldiers, killed one of them, stampeded the others, and made their escape to the mountains.

Scott sent for the white man, Thomas, who was the Indians' most trusted friend, and authorized him to seek out the leader, Utsala, and propose to him that if he would seize Charley and the others concerned in the "murder," and deliver them to headquarters for punishment, the General would call off the pursuit, secure a respite for the main body of refugees, and use his influence in Washington to get a special dispensation permitting the band to remain unmolested in their hills.

Thomas accepted the commission. With one or two Indian guides he made his way over secret paths to Utsala's hiding place. Here he stated his mission, and agreed with the chief that if the chief Tsala and his few companions were delivered to

justice there was good hope that the Government would make an exception in favor of the band of Lufty and allow them to remain in their own country.

Utsala's heart was bitter, for his wife and little son had starved to death on the mountain side. "But he thought of the thousands who were already on their long march into exile, and then he looked around upon his little band of followers. If only they might stay, even though a few must be sacrificed, it was better than that all should die—for they had sworn never to leave their country. He consented, and Thomas returned to report to General Scott."

There are various and conflicting tales about the Charley episode, some of them mere legends, evidently colored by prejudice, and others the recollections of very old people who were not actors in the event. On the other hand Mr. Mooney got the story directly from Colonel Thomas himself, and from Wasituna, Charley's youngest son, who alone was spared by General Scott on account of his youth. His relation can be accepted as historic fact.

"It was known that Charley and his party were hiding in a cave of the Great Smokies, at the head of Deep Creek." (There is no real cave in that region, but there are shelving rocks sufficient to shelter a few men, and that is what is evidently meant). "But it was not thought likely that he could be taken without bloodshed and a further delay which might prejudice the whole undertaking. Thomas determined to go to him and try to persuade him to come in and surrender.

"Declining Scott's offer of an escort, he went alone to the cave, and, getting between the Indians and their guns as they were sitting around the fire near the entrance, he walked up to Charley and announced his message. The old man listened in silence and then said simply, 'I will come in. I don't want to be hunted down by my own people.'"

"By command of General Scott, Charley, his brother, and the two elder sons were shot near the mouth of Tuckaseegee, a detachment of Cherokee prisoners being compelled to do the shooting in order to impress upon the prisoners the fact of their utter helplessness."

A year later (September 12, 1839) the Commissioner of Indian Affairs reported that the Indians scattered through the mountains of North Carolina and Tennessee numbered 1,046. They were in a distressing condition, mere landless aliens, staying under respite that might be cancelled any moment, and kept alive mostly by the white settlers out of pity or in return for labor they performed. If they had been left to their own devices it is more than probable that they would have been gradually gathered up and sent to join their brethren in the West. In fact a commissioner was appointed in the Spring of 1840 to enroll them for such removal.

But Colonel Thomas went to Washington, and stayed there continuously for three years, working with all the energy of a devoted friend to induce the Government to let the Eastern band remain in its old home and to secure for them their fair share of moneys due for reservations and improvements confiscated. And he succeeded.

In 1846, the Eastern Cherokees were admitted to participation in the benefits of the treaty of 1835, and Thomas was authorized at various times to buy back from the whites enough land in western North Carolina to serve as a permanent home for the Band. This he did: but since the State of North Carolina persisted in refusing to recognize Indians as landowners, until 1866, Thomas held the deeds in his own name, as their authorized agent under the Government. The Indian title was finally adjudicated by the United States during the period from 1875 to 1894.

The present legal status of the Eastern Band of Cherokees is indeterminate and anomalous. It has been ruled by the courts that they are citizens of the United States, and again that they were wards of the Government. They are under discipline of a resident Indian agent, but never have been reservation Indians. They are citizens of North Carolina, and at the same time a body corporate and politic. They have a tribal constitution, and are governed in

"By command of General Scott, Charley, his

the mouth of Tuckaseegee,

a detachment of Cherokee prison

in order to impress upon the prisone

...nd the two elder sons were shot near

...eing compelled to do the shooting
...e fact of their utter helplessness."

tribal matters by chiefs and councillors elected by themselves.

Their lands were purchased by themselves, or by the Government from funds due them, but they cannot make free contracts nor alienate the lands that they hold in severalty. They pay taxes, except poll tax, perform road service, and are amenable to the local courts, save in land matters. Male Cherokees of voting age who can read and write English are allowed to vote—sometimes, and sometimes not.

There are about 1,800 of these Indians in the Qualla boundary, and about 500 more scattered in other parts of North Carolina. More than half of them are fullbloods, a much larger percentage than among their kinsmen in Oklahoma.*

Nearly all of the men, and many of the women, can read and write their own language. About half of them can use enough English for ordinary intercourse. The Government training school at Cherokee postoffice affords an excellent education to the boys and girls, and, under the present Superintendent, is doing fine work among the adults by demonstrating modern methods of farming and stock raising.

The prompt and generous response of the Eastern Cherokees to our Government's calls for subscriptions to liberty bonds and war savings stamps was surprising and delightful. In proportion to their ability they more than equalled the whites. Their young men went into the war willingly and fought gallantly. Only one slacker was reported in the whole tribe, and he was immediately brought to book by his own people. The Indian children in the Cherokee school are supporting a war orphan in France.

The sacrifice of poor old Tsali and his kinmen was not made in vain.

---

* Approximate figures for 2000: 9,000 in Qualla boundary, 13,000 in other parts of state, and 15 percent fullbloods.

Author Horace Kephart

both chronicled and made history in the

Great Smoky Mountains.

Design and illustation by Joey Heath
Photo credits:
John Ross is from a lithograph published by McKenney and Hall in *The Indian Tribes of North America,* 1836-1844, based on a painting made in 1835, artist unknown.
All other photos are courtesy of the Museum of the Cherokees